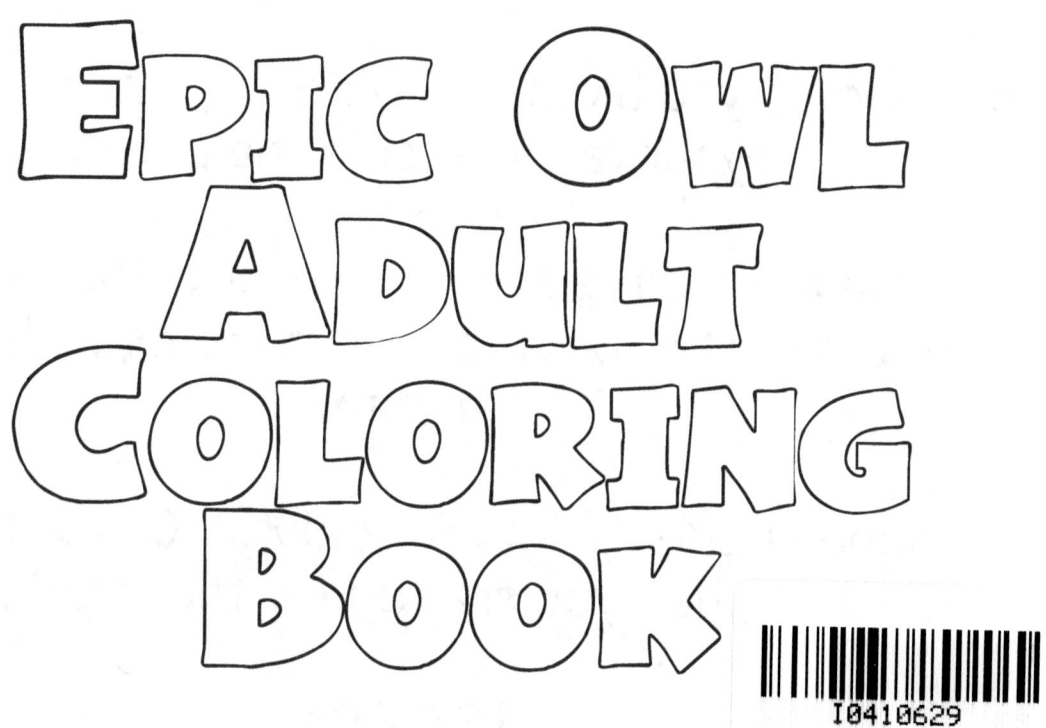

Epic Owl Adult Coloring Book

BY SUSAN POTTERFIELDS

ISBN: 10: 1540340139
ISBN- 13: 978-1540340139

I0410629

How would you like to be able to print off copies of your favorite coloring books?

How about having access to over a 1000's coloring books for the price of one coloring book every month.

Coupon Code to Join for only $1.00 for the first month when you sign up for the mailing list.

TRYTODAY

www.digitalcoloringbooks.com

Susan Potterfields is a digital artist. You can find more of her work on Amazon and digitalcoloringbooks.com.